Original title:
The Orchestra of Odd Feelings

Copyright © 2024 Creative Arts Management OÜ
All rights reserved.

Author: Adeline Fairfax
ISBN HARDBACK: 978-9916-90-792-4
ISBN PAPERBACK: 978-9916-90-793-1

Echoes of Fleeting Moments

In the whisper of twilight's glow,
Memories dance, soft and slow.
Fleeting shadows brush the ground,
In silence, lost moments are found.

Time slips through like grains of sand,
Each second held in a gentle hand.
Echoes call from days gone by,
A fleeting sigh, a wistful cry.

In the heart where secrets lay,
Moments linger, then drift away.
Yet, in the stillness of the night,
Fleeting dreams take their flight.

Tomorrow's dawn will soon arrive,
With echoes that will surely thrive.
In every heartbeat, every breath,
We cherish life beyond all death.

The Ballad of Buried Realities

Beneath the surface, voices stir,
Whispers of truth that never were.
Hidden tales in shadows creep,
As the world spins, secrets sleep.

Once vibrant dreams lie wrapped in clay,
Faded colors in shades of gray.
A haunting melody fills the air,
The ballad sings of what we bear.

Echoes lost in muffled cries,
Fragmented glances, long goodbyes.
Through tangled roots, our truths entwine,
Buried realities softly shine.

Yet through the fog, a flicker glows,
Hope awakens as the heart knows.
From the shadows, we'll arise,
To weave our song beneath the skies.

Lullabies of Lost Connections

In the cradle of the night,
Lullabies drift in silver light.
Once shared dreams now fade away,
In the silence, shadows sway.

Fingers touch but hearts retreat,
Fractured ties, a bittersweet.
Words unspoken linger long,
In the stillness, a silent song.

Time flows onward, rivers wide,
Carrying love that cannot hide.
Yet somewhere in the quiet space,
Lullabies of loss embrace.

When the stars begin to gleam,
We hold onto a fragile dream.
In every note, there lies a plea,
To sing of what we used to be.

Nocturne for the Anxious Soul

In the stillness, shadows loom,
The heart beats loud in the hush of gloom.
Thoughts collide, a wild race,
In the dark, we find our place.

Moonlight casts a tender glow,
Illuminating what we know.
A serenade for restless minds,
In the quiet, solace finds.

Whispers of fear in the night,
Yet hope lingers, soft and bright.
Through the chaos, still we strive,
In this nocturne, we revive.

As dawn creeps near, we take a breath,
With every dawn, there's life, not death.
In our hearts, the music plays,
A soothing balm through endless days.

Dissonant Dreams

In shadows where the silence falls,
A symphony of echoes calls.
Fragments of a night untold,
Woven in the dreams of old.

Drifting through a painted haze,
Lost in an uncharted maze.
Voices clash in muted screams,
Awakening the dissonant dreams.

Melodies from a Chaotic Mind

Whispers swirl in crowded space,
Thoughts collide, a frenzied race.
Notes that clash and yet combine,
 Creating melodies divine.

In chaos lies a hidden tune,
A rhythm dancing with the moon.
Fleeting moments, lost and found,
 In the chaos, beauty's crowned.

The Soundtrack of Unspoken Thoughts

In every glance, a story spins,
Silent words where language thins.
The heartbeats play a quiet chord,
In the silence, life is stored.

Echoes linger in the air,
Feelings woven through a stare.
Each unsaid word a gentle plea,
The soundtrack of what cannot be.

Rhythms of Restless Souls

In restless nights when shadows creep,
The soul stirs wide awake from sleep.
A pulse beneath the quiet skin,
Awakening the doubts within.

Footsteps echo on the ground,
Searching for a place unbound.
Rhythms of the heart collide,
In restless dreams where hopes abide.

The Fugue of Faint Smiles

In shadows deep where secrets lie,
Whispers brush the evening sky.
Faint smiles flicker, lost in time,
A melody of forgotten rhyme.

Echoes dance on weary beams,
Carried forth on tender dreams.
Each note a ghost, a fleeting sigh,
The pain of joy we can't deny.

With every glance, a story frays,
In silent corners, love decays.
Yet still we hope, we softly swell,
In this fugue, we weave our spell.

So let the smiles, though faint, remain,
A bittersweet, enduring pain.
For in their depth, our hearts entwine,
A fleeting waltz, a tender line.

Psalm of the Pensive Heart

In quiet hours where shadows brood,
The heart reflects in solitude.
Each thump a prayer, a silent plea,
For solace found in memory.

The pages turn, yet stories freeze,
A tapestry of hopes and pleas.
Riddled with doubt, yet still we seek,
In pensive whispers, we grow weak.

But let the ink of pain be known,
For in this ache, we are not alone.
A psalm unwinds, a gentle art,
The weary beats of every heart.

And when the dawn breaks soft and bright,
The pensive heart finds its own light.
In all the questions, answers blend,
A prayerful song that will not end.

A Waltz with Wistfulness

Beneath the stars, we gently sway,
In wistful dreams, we lose our way.
A dance of sighs, a breath apart,
Each step a whisper of the heart.

With every turn, the shadows blend,
A spiral path that feels like friends.
The music hums of days gone by,
A waltz beneath the midnight sky.

Her laughter lingers in the air,
A bittersweet, enchanting snare.
In twilight's grasp, we softly twine,
Two souls adrift, in thought's design.

Yet as we dance, the dream must fade,
Each wistful glance, a memory made.
A fleeting tune, a tender call,
In the waltz of life, we risk it all.

Resonance of Ruined Expectations

In shattered hopes, the echoes ring,
Ruined dreams that time won't bring.
A resonance of whispered fears,
The quiet toll of bygone years.

Each choice we made, a path unreal,
A collage formed from hollow feel.
Yet in this ruin, we still stand,
Building castles in the sand.

The weight of wishes hangs like fog,
Lost in the maze, we drag the dog.
But through the mist, a light appears,
A flicker bright that dries our tears.

In every ruin, there's a spark,
A chance to rise from the deep dark.
For though expectations may not thrive,
In ruined dreams, our hopes revive.

The Harmony of Hushed Cries

In shadows where the secrets dwell,
Soft echoes weave a tender spell.
Silent whispers dance in the night,
Beneath the stars, their hearts take flight.

A gentle breeze carries the sound,
Of dreams that linger, lost but found.
In every sigh, a story spun,
The harmony of souls as one.

Moonlit pathways guide their way,
Where unspoken words softly play.
Together in this sacred space,
Hushed cries find their warm embrace.

With every breath, a bond so dear,
United by the love they share.
In the stillness, they softly rise,
Awakening the beauty in hushes and sighs.

Harmony of Unseen Echoes

In the stillness where light meets dark,
A melody forms, tender and stark.
Unseen echoes whisper and blend,
Creating a song that knows no end.

Through the cracks of reality's hold,
Lives the warmth of stories untold.
With each pulse, the heart will sing,
Harmonizing with everything.

The waves of time ripple and flow,
As secrets awaken from deep below.
In the quiet, life's threads entwine,
Unseen echoes, pure and divine.

As shadows melt into the light,
Harmony blooms, a glorious sight.
In the silence, find sweet release,
In unseen echoes, discover peace.

Whispers in the Strings of Emotion

Gentle threads of feeling sway,
In a tapestry of night and day.
Each whisper builds a fragile tone,
In the heart's orchestra, we are not alone.

From laughter to tears, the notes arise,
Resounding softly beneath the skies.
In every chord, a story lives,
Whispers weaving what love gives.

Strings of hope, pulled tight with care,
Vibrate softly in the air.
In the silence, a world ignites,
With whispers that reach extraordinary heights.

Through the echoes of joy and pain,
The strings of emotion, never in vain.
Together they sing, forever true,
A harmony painted in every hue.

Crescendo of the Surreal Heart

In the twilight where dreams collide,
Surreal wonders come alive inside.
A crescendo rises, wild and free,
The heartbeat of all that's meant to be.

Colors swirl in a passionate dance,
An explosion of rhythm, a fleeting glance.
In whispers of magic, skies ignite,
Creating moments that feel so right.

The heart beats strong with every rise,
Unfolding mysteries, silent cries.
In this symphony of dark and bright,
The surreal heart takes its flight.

Echoes of laughter, shadows of tears,
A cacophony calming all fears.
In the harmony of what's absurd,
The crescendo sings, unspoken, unheard.

The Crescendo of Complicated Feelings

A heart that beats in disarray,
Whispers lost in the fray.
Moments dance, then fade away,
Emotions swell, night and day.

Twists and turns, a winding road,
Secrets heavy, a silent load.
In shadows cast, the truth erodes,
Yet hope ignites, a bright abode.

Questions linger, insight delayed,
Fading dreams, paths mislaid.
Yet through the chaos, light is played,
A symphony of love displayed.

In every heart, a tale unfolds,
Layers deep, the silence holds.
Amidst the clash, a truth so bold,
The crescendo of feelings, manifold.

Nocturne of Uncertainty

Beneath the stars, a muted night,
Whispers of doubt take flight.
Chasing shadows, seeking light,
In the stillness, fear ignites.

Thoughts like clouds, they gather fast,
Moments fleeting, shadows cast.
Hopes that wane, and dreams that last,
Drifting softly, like a past.

The moon gazes with knowing eyes,
Illuminating hidden sighs.
In the silence, truth can rise,
Yet in this dark, uncertainty lies.

A song of night, both sweet and grim,
Tales of doubt on the whim.
Yet in the dark, the stars still brim,
Holding fast to dreams within.

Orchestral Anxieties

In the hall, instruments clash,
Strings pulled tight with unseen thrash.
Drumbeats echo, a heart's race,
Melodies lost in the space.

Fingers tremble on keys of fate,
Winds whisper secrets, dreams that grate.
Tension swells in the gathered crowd,
Anxiety wraps like a shroud.

Conductor's wand calls forth the sound,
Yet in silence, fears abound.
Crescendo of worries takes flight,
In harmonies dark, shadows ignite.

Notes collide, a storm within,
The beauty found where fears begin.
In this orchestral dance of dread,
Life's symphony plays on, well-bred.

Discordant Daydreams

Visions tumble, colors clash,
Thoughts alight in a frantic flash.
Reality bends, whispers shout,
In dreams, new paths twist about.

Clouds drip rain in hues of gray,
Waves of thought drift far away.
Joy turned jarring, peace a scream,
Fractured mirrors reflect a dream.

Whirling thoughts like autumn leaves,
In the chaos, the spirit grieves.
Echoes dance in the mind's dark maze,
Discord blooms in the brightest praise.

Yet within the noise, a soft hum found,
Hope flickers, unbound.
In the heart, a gentle plea,
To dream in tones of harmony.

Notes from the Edge of Reality

Faint whispers on the cusp of light,
Reality drifts into the night.
Edges blur with each passing glance,
Unraveling tight threads of chance.

Thoughts like echoes, fleeting and sly,
Questioning truths that never die.
Moments collide, time bends and sways,
Footsteps linger in dream's soft haze.

Peering through cracks in the known,
To worlds where wild imaginations are sown.
Fraying ropes tied to what we see,
Uncertain futures dance to be free.

Each note whispers of paths untread,
Fictions woven, lies in the thread.
From the edge, let the journey begin,
In the space where dreaming starts to spin.

Crescendos of Curiosity

In the still, a question explodes,
Wonders sprout in scattered codes.
Unexpected twists invite the bold,
Curiosity, a treasure to hold.

Through the maze of the unknown,
Seeds of wonder are clearly sown.
Chasing shadows, seeking the light,
In every puzzle, new insights ignite.

Notes of inquiry rise and swell,
Each discovery, a vibrant bell.
Fearing nothing, seeking more,
Crescendos sound as spirits soar.

With each clue, the heart expands,
Life unfolds in open hands.
In every corner, secrets tease,
Curiosity dances in the breeze.

Vagabond Vibes

On roads untraveled, I roam so free,
With dreams as my compass, the sky's the sea.
Each sunset whispers a tale in the air,
While stars guide my heart, with tender care.

Footprints in sand, stories untold,
I chase the horizon, as the night turns cold.
The wind sings my name, a familiar song,
In the dance of the wild, I know I belong.

Journeys expand in the paths we make,
With every step forward, fears start to break.
Strangers become friends in twilight's embrace,
In the fleeting moments, we all find our place.

So here's to the wanderers, hearts full of fire,
Chasing the echoes of dreams that inspire.
For life is a canvas, and we are the art,
With vagabond vibes, we wander, we part.

The Disarrayed Waltz

In a room full of shadows, we twirl and sway,
Steps out of rhythm, but we find our way.
With laughter and tears, our hearts intertwine,
In the chaos of love, we're perfectly aligned.

The music's a puzzle, discordant yet sweet,
With every misstep, we regain our beat.
Through the moments of doubt in this frantic trance,
We twine through the disarrayed waltz of chance.

Eyes closed to the world, lost in the dance,
Navigating stormy seas with a glance.
Each turn tells a story, a secret unveiled,
In the chaos of movement, our fears are exhaled.

As the night fades away, we bow to the light,
Two souls intertwining, bold and upright.
With grace in our hearts, we take a last chance,
In the disarrayed waltz, we found romance.

Emotions in Abandon

Left behind faces, a canvas in time,
Brush strokes of heartache, love's silent rhyme.
In corners of memory, feelings reside,
Emotions in abandon, where secrets confide.

Whispers of laughter chase shadows away,
Tears craft the rivers where dreams used to play.
With every heartbeat, an echo remains,
A symphony forged in joy and in pains.

Unraveled connections, the threads made anew,
In the chaos of silence, I still think of you.
Each moment a testament, wild and profound,
In the depths of abandonment, love can be found.

So here's to the feelings we dare to ignore,
To embrace the chaos, we find so much more.
Amongst all the ruins, in twilight's soft glow,
Emotions in abandon, forever will flow.

The Flutter of Fractured Dances

In gardens of twilight, where shadows entwine,
Fractured our steps, yet the rhythm divine.
Fluttering hearts in the soft evening breeze,
We dance through the chaos, our souls feel at ease.

Each turn is a puzzle, a twist in the night,
With laughter as lanterns, we chase down the light.
In the flutter of moments, lost in the trance,
We find our own meaning within every dance.

The music may waver, but we won't let go,
In the swirl of uncertainty, our spirits will grow.
With every misstep that leads to a smile,
Fractured yet beautiful, we dance every mile.

So here in the twilight, with friends by my side,
We'll weave through the night, let our hearts be our guide.

For within the disarray, we find our stance,
In the flutter of fractured dances, we take our chance.

Lunatic Sonatas

In shadows deep, the visions play,
A dance of thoughts, both night and day.
Moonlit whispers call my name,
In this wild tune, I feel no shame.

The notes collide, they twist and turn,
In fevered dreams, I feel the burn.
A symphony of reckless grace,
A madman's waltz in empty space.

Delirium wraps its arms around,
In each sonata, chaos found.
Music flows like raging tides,
In lunacy, my spirit rides.

The Distortion of a Serene Mind

Calm waters shimmer under the sun,
Yet shadows creep, the battle's begun.
A tranquil heart, a fractured thread,
Where light once reigned, now fears are bred.

Thoughts spiral down in winding roads,
Serenity falters, burdened loads.
Stillness shatters, pieces collide,
In the quiet depths, I must decide.

Voices murmur, truths feel wrong,
The light I seek is a distant song.
Amidst the noise, I search for peace,
But in distortion, fears increase.

Echoes of Uncertainty

Whispers hover in the air,
Questions linger, stripped bare.
In the silence, doubts arise,
A haunting gaze, a maze of lies.

Each echo fades, then comes again,
In the shadows, I feel the strain.
Chasing answers, I lose my way,
In this reverberating fray.

The heartbeats shift, the rhythm's wrong,
Each pulse a note in an aching song.
Clarity dances just out of sight,
In uncertainty's grip, I seek the light.

Chaotic Compositions

Scattered notes across the floor,
Melodies clash, then roar.
Frantic strokes on canvas wide,
In chaos, my dreams confide.

Every stroke tells a tale untold,
Vivid colors, notions bold.
Life's complexity, a tangled thread,
In chaos, all my fears are fed.

Abstract visions haunt my mind,
In every piece, what will I find?
Creation bursts in wild release,
In chaotic compositions, I find peace.

The Diagonal Dance of Dissonance

In shadows twist the silent cries,
A melody that feels askew.
Steps out of sync with whispered lies,
A rhythm lost, not breaking through.

The angles shift, a fractured beat,
Confusion spins in measured grace.
Each turn, a battle, bitter sweet,
In chaos finds a fleeting place.

Unraveled chords in tangled air,
Disjointed hues of vibrant sound.
Yet in the clash, a spark laid bare,
In dissonance, a truth is found.

The diagonal sway, a mirrored plight,
Where harmony and discord blend.
A dance of shadows, void of light,
Yet in this fray, we learn to mend.

Whirls of Nostalgic Noise

In echoes of a distant song,
A time long past, yet lingering near.
Dreams wrapped tight, where hearts belong,
In whispered winds, the memories cheer.

The clock ticks back, a spiral spin,
As laughter weaves through dusky skies.
With every note, the tales begin,
And in the din, true essence lies.

Each whisper holds a gift of old,
A dance of moments, sweet and bright.
The warmth of times forever told,
In whirls of noise, we find our light.

Through fleeting frames of silver hue,
Where shadows blend with vibrant sound.
Nostalgia's touch, an art so true,
In every swirl, our hearts abound.

Fractured Finale

The curtain falls on fractured dreams,
A symphony of broken lines.
Each note a tale, a whispered scream,
In silence lost, the heart resigns.

The last refrain, a shattering spark,
As shadows dance in fading light.
An echo guides through realms so dark,
Where hopes once soared, now fade from sight.

Yet in the cracks, a glow persists,
A tender pulse beneath the weight.
Through deepest night, a flicker twists,
In fractured tunes, we celebrate.

The end may come, but not in vain,
For in the shards, a strength to rise.
From fractured paths, we bear the pain,
And find our way through tangled skies.

Pulse of Perplexity

In tangled webs of thought we weave,
Where questions spin in endless chase.
Each heartbeat whispers, then deceives,
A puzzling dance we can't quite face.

The rhythm shifts, a curious beat,
As clarity slips through our hands.
In chaos lies a truth discreet,
Where wandering mind forever stands.

Through corridors of doubt we roam,
In shadows cast by fleeting light.
The pulse of thought, it calls us home,
Yet leaves us lost in endless night.

With every step, a layer peels,
Unraveling the depths we seek.
In perplexity, the heart reveals,
The beauty found in moments weak.

The Ballad of Jumbled Joys

In a world where laughter blends,
Whispers dance on breezy bends.
Colors swirl in vibrant hues,
Each moment sparkles like morning dew.

Hearts collide, a joyous sound,
In messy streets where love is found.
Simple pleasures, sweet and rare,
Echo softly through the air.

Gathered dreams, a tapestry,
Weaving tales of harmony.
In every glance, a story shared,
In jumbled joys, we are ensnared.

Through tangled paths, we make our way,
Finding music in the fray.
In every misstep, every choice,
Resides the magic, hear the voice.

Cauldron of Chords

In the depths of night, we play,
Strings vibrate, come what may.
Notes caress the shadows long,
In this cauldron, we belong.

Melodies swirl in a lively brew,
Mixing dreams, both old and new.
Fingers dance on frets with grace,
Creating rhythms, time and space.

Each chord struck, a heartbeat shared,
In harmony, our souls are bared.
Sparks of sound ignite the air,
In this cauldron, our hearts laid bare.

Lost in the magic of each refrain,
We find solace in the rain.
Through every strum, we craft our fate,
In a symphony, love resonates.

Trills of the Unraveled

In unison, our voices rise,
Fractured notes, unmask the skies.
Dissonance, a song of hope,
In every fall, we learn to cope.

Whispers thread through tangled dreams,
Fleeting moments, silent screams.
The world unwinds, a ballad spun,
In every shadow, shines the sun.

Trills of laughter, tears entwined,
A journey mapped in heart and mind.
Though we stray on winding roads,
We find a way to share our loads.

Amidst the chaos, beauty waits,
In every heart, love advocates.
With every stumble, every flaw,
We rise again, bring forth true awe.

Brightness Amidst Dissonance

In a cacophony of sound,
Light emerges from underground.
Fragments clash, yet still we find,
In dissonance, our hearts aligned.

Glimmers flash through darkened skies,
Hope ignites with every rise.
Through jarring notes, a spark is drawn,
A symphony of a brand new dawn.

In shadows thick, we grasp and cling,
To fleeting joy that music brings.
Embrace the chaos, feel the thrill,
In every discord, magic fills.

Together we sing, hand in hand,
Creating warmth in disordered land.
For even in storms, we choose to see,
Brightness blooms where hearts are free.

Serenade of the Misunderstood

In shadows cast by silent dreams,
They wander lost in muted streams.
Voices soft, yet hearts ablaze,
In solitude, their spirits graze.

Whispers linger in the night,
Yearning for a fleeting light.
Each tear speaks a tale untold,
Of love and loss, both brave and bold.

In corners where the laughter fades,
They craft their hope in whispered shades.
A melody that tastes like pain,
Yet still they dance within the rain.

Through tangled paths of doubt and fear,
They find a refuge, holding near.
With every note, their truth will flow,
A serenade for hearts that know.

Baroque Unrest

In gilded halls where shadows loom,
The echoes of a restless gloom.
A tapestry of voices clash,
As beauty fades beneath the brash.

Each corner holds a tale concealed,
Of artistry that once revealed.
But all the colors bleed and fade,
Where once the finest dreams were laid.

As instruments of chaos play,
The cadence leads the heart astray.
A symphony of time's disdain,
Where sorrow drowns the joy in vain.

Yet in the discord, sparks ignite,
Rebellion born from faded light.
For in the turmoil, truth may rise,
And paint anew the boundless skies.

Beneath the Crescendo of Confusion

Amidst the clamor, thoughts collide,
Where clarity has often died.
In rattled minds, the tempests brew,
A song of chaos, bright yet blue.

The notes entwine, a wild chase,
Each search for peace, a restless race.
With every rise, another fall,
A dance of silence, heed the call.

They sink in pools of swirling doubt,
Where once resided hope, now clout.
But in the heart of disarray,
A flicker waits to light the way.

So breathe the storm, embrace the fray,
For from confusion blooms the day.
Beneath the shouts, a whisper strays,
A truth that quietly obeys.

Echoes of the Discontented

In the void where dreams once stood,
Resounds the grief of lost and good.
The shadows stretch with aching sighs,
As fleeting moments slip and die.

With every pulse, regret's refrain,
The echoes weave a haunting chain.
In silence thick as winter's breath,
They dance with memories of death.

Yet hope, a ghost, remains in view,
To spark a fire, to start anew.
Though discontent may fill the air,
A whisper dares to still despair.

So let the echoes rise and swell,
For in the depths, there lies a bell.
A call to strength, a fleeting chance,
To break the chain, to dare to dance.

Interlude of Irregular Joys

In fleeting moments, laughter blooms,
Bright as the sun through winter's glooms.
Strange whispers float on gentle air,
A dance of joy, both light and rare.

Soft shadows blend with colors bright,
Undefined dreams take wing at night.
Surprises stir the quiet soul,
In these odd joys, we feel whole.

Beneath the stars, our spirits play,
In rhythms strange, we find our way.
The heart embraces what is true,
In every change, a pulse anew.

Moments weave like threads of gold,
Each one a story, yet untold.
With every beat, we laugh and sigh,
In irregular joys, we learn to fly.

Tones of the Timid Heart

Upon the edge of whispered dreams,
The timid heart softly gleams.
In shadows cast by fears that stay,
A silent song begins to play.

Each note a tremor, tender, shy,
In delicate echoes, breaths comply.
Hushed melodies float on the breeze,
Embracing doubts, seeking to please.

Within the quiet, courage grows,
As secret streams of passion flow.
In fragile hues, the heart finds spark,
Tones of the timid dance in the dark.

Unseen yet felt, the rhythm starts,
A symphony springs from timid hearts.
In every pulse, a chance to rise,
With every breath, the spirit flies.

Cimmerian Chords

In the depth where shadows blend,
Cimmerian chords begin to descend.
A haunting strum of lost delight,
Echoing dreams that fade from sight.

Whispers of night beneath the moon,
Melodies linger, a soft croon.
Darkness cradles the heart's refrain,
In every silence, a ghostly pain.

Yet in the gloom, a flicker stays,
A spark of light in misty haze.
These chords entwine, a velvet grasp,
Holding the sorrow with gentle clasp.

From shadows rise, the music calls,
In Cimmerian depths, the spirit sprawls.
With every strum, the night will end,
A journey lost, yet to transcend.

Fantasia of Fleeting Feelings

In colors bright that swiftly pass,
Fantasia dances on the grass.
With every heartbeat, feelings soar,
A wondrous glimpse of something more.

Transitory, like summer rain,
Each drop a joy, a hint of pain.
In whispers soft, the moments blend,
A tapestry we cannot mend.

Like butterflies that kiss the flame,
Fleeting feelings, never the same.
In their embrace, we taste the bliss,
A gentle sigh, a soft, sweet kiss.

Yet in their wake, the echoes stay,
Reminding us of love's ballet.
In every moment, short yet bright,
Fantasia glimmers, a fleeting light.

Dissonance in the Quiet Spaces

In corners where silence has stayed,
Whispers collide, emotions invade.
Fleeting echoes of unspoken words,
Drowning in stillness, unheard, unheard.

The heartbeats sync with the ticking clock,
Waves of tension that cannot unlock.
Beneath calm faces, turmoil brews,
In the calm of the night, truth misconstrues.

The air thickens with unvoiced fears,
As shadows of doubt draw near.
Silent cries that slice through the dark,
A struggle of souls, a flickering spark.

In quiet spaces, the noise will rise,
A symphony born from concealed sighs.
Dissonance dances in every breath,
Finding its way amidst life and death.

Reverberations of Unease

Under the surface, tremors quake,
Each thought a ripple, a stone in the lake.
Questions echo where answers should be,
Filling the void, a haunting decree.

The shadows cast by the flickering light,
Reveal the fears that hide from sight.
In whispered tones, they start to grow,
A melody of worry, a dissonant flow.

The world spins softly, yet feels so loud,
An unseen shroud wraps round the crowd.
In every glance, a story untold,
Leaving hearts heavy, yet feeling bold.

Through the murmurs, an urgency stirs,
With reverberations, anxiety purrs.
Unraveling threads in a fabric of dreams,
Each note of unease, or so it seems.

A Serenade of Shadows

Beneath the moon, where the silence sighs,
Shadows gather, and whispers rise.
In their embrace, lost hopes dwell,
Each flicker a story, a soft farewell.

Night wraps tightly in its velvet seam,
Drifting softly through a forgotten dream.
With every rustle, a heart skips pace,
A dance of twilight, a lover's chase.

The starlight flickers, intentions obscure,
A serenade gentle, yet so unsure.
With every hushed breath, secrets unfold,
In the realm of shadows, hearts feel bold.

In twilight's grasp, where the lost find grace,
Echoes of longing in time and space.
A serenade calling, sweet and profound,
In every shadow, love can be found.

The Unseen Conductor's Touch

In silence, the strings begin to quiver,
An unseen hand makes the tension shiver.
Notes tremble lightly, like a soft breeze,
Guiding the chaos, bringing it ease.

With gentle gestures, the rhythm sways,
Leading the hearts in delicate plays.
Through subtle movements, the tempo sparks,
Creating a symphony in hidden arcs.

Each sound a whisper, a secret shared,
The depth of feeling, so deeply paired.
In the concert of life, emotions blend,
An unseen conductor, our souls to mend.

In the quiet, the magic unfolds,
The unseen touch, a story retold.
Through the melodies, connection flows,
In the silence, our essence grows.

Cadence of the Unwary

Stepping softly on the grass,
Whispers echo, moments pass.
Shadows dance beneath the trees,
Chasing dreams upon the breeze.

Footsteps falter, hearts aglow,
In the twilight, secrets flow.
Lost in thoughts of what might be,
Eyes wide open, yet not free.

Unseen rhythms sway the mind,
In their grasp, the lost unwind.
Fleeting visions brush our skin,
Tangled tales where dreams begin.

With each heartbeat, chances stir,
In the silence, voices blur.
Cadence calls, but we must tread,
Through the paths where fears are fed.

Unraveled in Symphony

Strings of fate in harmony,
Notes entwined in ecstasy.
Melodies weave through the air,
Echoing shadows everywhere.

Each refrain, a story told,
Whispers of the brave and bold.
Laughter mingles with the sighs,
In the cadence, love defies.

Chords that break and yet unite,
In this dance of day and night.
Fractured moments stitched with care,
Unraveled dreams hang in the air.

In the silence, whispers dwell,
Echoes of a magic spell.
Symphony of hearts that blend,
In this song, we find a friend.

Fragmented Harmonies

Notes collide, a disarray,
Fragments of a grand bouquet.
In the chaos, beauty lies,
Shattered sounds and faded cries.

Torn between the light and dark,
Each collision, each remark.
Melodies lost in the fray,
Yet somehow find their own way.

Harmonies that tease the mind,
In the wreckage, we might find.
Shards of love and hope revive,
In the ruin, we survive.

Through the mess, the music plays,
Finding peace in disarray.
Fragmented but never gone,
In the silence, we hold on.

The Sound of Halos and Hiccups

Whispers of the night take flight,
Halos gleam in muted light.
Hiccups break the gentle calm,
In the shadows, there's a balm.

Echoes of a laughter sweet,
Ringing softly, feel the beat.
Innocence woven with care,
In this dance, we're stripped bare.

Voice of angels, soft yet near,
In their song, we lose our fear.
Halos flicker in the dark,
Hiccups play their joyful spark.

Resonance of the purest heart,
In the ending, we restart.
Sound of life, both light and deep,
In our dreams, the angels sleep.

The Vibrato of Vulnerability

In the quiet hum of night,
Whispers coil like smoke.
Each note a tender flight,
Echoes of the unspoke.

Hearts reveal their hidden scars,
Bare beneath the moon's glow.
Floating like distant stars,
Fragile, yet they bestow.

In trembling hands, we find grace,
A melody soft and true.
Seeking warmth in this space,
Where we dare to break through.

With every breath we sing loud,
Vulnerability's embrace.
Standing strong amid the crowd,
Finding strength in our place.

Shattered Scores

Notes fell like broken glass,
Melodies lost in despair.
Each rhythm a shadowed pass,
Fragments cast in the air.

Silent echoes linger near,
Haunting the hearts of the brave.
In the silence, we hear fear,
Cries of those who won't save.

Time rewinds the bloodied sheets,
Tales of battles fought alone.
Yet within our aching beats,
Seeds of hope have been sown.

From the shards, a new song flows,
Rising from the ashes bright.
Healing where the sorrow grows,
In the darkness, we find light.

Unruly Harmonies

Discord dances in the air,
Notes clash in wild delight.
Chaotic beauty lays bare,
A symphony ignites.

Voices intertwine and blend,
Creating a tempest's roar.
Every phrase, a twist, a bend,
Darling chaos at its core.

Within the tumult, we find space,
To let loose our hidden grace.
Each moment, a wild embrace,
In the mess, we leave a trace.

Embrace the noise, let it soar,
Unruly chords that twist and twine.
In the clamor, we explore,
The beauty of the divine.

Soliloquy of Silences

In the pause between breaths,
Thoughts unfurl like gentle wings.
Stillness holds its own depths,
Speaking in silent springs.

Words unspoken linger long,
Wrapped in the tapestry of time.
Each quiet draws forth a song,
Echoes of love, loss, and rhyme.

In the hush, we find our place,
A sanctuary soft and pure.
Within the void, there's a grace,
An invitation to endure.

Silence speaks in whispers clear,
More profound than words could say.
In its heart, we lose our fear,
Finding peace in bright array.

The Discord of Forgotten Melodies

In shadows deep, the echoes cry,
Whispers lost, where dreams comply.
Melodies fade into the night,
Chasing ghosts of fleeting light.

A symphony of silent grief,
Notes that linger, yet bring no relief.
In every chord, a tale untold,
The heart's lament, forever bold.

Fingers dance on strings of woe,
Each pluck and strum, a hollow glow.
Forgotten tunes in twilight's breath,
Resonate with hints of death.

So listen close, to whispers past,
An orchestra of dreams amassed.
In dissonance, find truths concealed,
The forgotten songs, once revealed.

Prelude to a Misguided Journey

Beneath the stars, a path unwinds,
Guided by hope, yet lost in minds.
Each step forward, a cautious tread,
With shadows lurking, dreams misled.

Winds of chance weave through the trees,
Dancing lightly with the breeze.
A call to venture, brave yet stark,
Into the depths, where fears embark.

Maps of fate in hands uncertain,
Veils of doubt, a heavy burden.
The road ahead, both broad and narrow,
Carried forth by wings, yet sorrow.

In mirrored skies, the journey starts,
A tapestry woven from restless hearts.
With every choice, a path untold,
In the face of fear, courage bold.

The Sonic Palette of Distress

Colors swirl in sounds profound,
Each note a brushstroke, chaos found.
Crimson screams and azure sighs,
Harmony blooms where discord lies.

Rhythms pulse like racing hearts,
Echoing doubts, where darkness starts.
In vivid shades of grief and pain,
A canvas painted with disdain.

Cacophonies entwine the air,
An artist's voice is stripped and bare.
As sirens wail, the colors fade,
In sonic shades of dreams delayed.

Yet in this murky, tangled mess,
A beauty lies within distress.
For every loss, a vibrant claim,
A reenactment of the same.

Harmonies of Halcyon Hesitations

In tranquil tones, the whispers pause,
Caught in the throes of endless cause.
Fingers linger, yet fail to play,
Hesitation maps the way.

Golden rays of twilight glow,
Capture moments like falling snow.
In stillness, hearts learn to abide,
A gentle tide, a rolling ride.

The echoes whisper soft and low,
Rotating dreams in ebb and flow.
With every breath, a chance deferred,
In graceful waits, the soul is stirred.

So let the music find its breath,
In time, we learn the art of rest.
For in each note of pause, we find,
The harmony of heart and mind.

Interludes of Introspection

In the quiet depths I see,
Whispers of the soul's decree.
Thoughts dance like shadows cast,
Echoes of a fleeting past.

Moments linger in the haze,
Lost within a reflective phase.
Questions rise like morning dew,
Unfolding layers, old and new.

Fleeting time, a river flows,
In its currents, wisdom grows.
I find peace in stillness found,
Within these interludes, I'm bound.

Here, the heart lays bare its song,
A melody, both sweet and strong.
In every silence, dreams arise,
Interludes beneath the skies.

The Overture of Uncertainty

A stage set with doubt and fear,
Curtains drawn, the path unclear.
Voices clash with fervent might,
Whispers lost to the fading light.

Each decision a delicate thread,
Woven stories of what lies ahead.
In the stillness, futures play,
An overture of night and day.

Questions dance on a cresting wave,
Caught between the bold and brave.
To embrace the unknown, we strive,
In uncertainty, we come alive.

Yet within the chaos, a spark,
A guiding light in the dark.
Holding hope, we move along,
An overture, a timeless song.

Timbral Trails of Tenderness

Softly tread on paths of grace,
Where echoes leave a warm embrace.
Gentle notes of love unwind,
In every moment, peace we find.

Whispers carried on the breeze,
Tender tales that aim to please.
In the symphony of hearts,
Timbral trails of warmth imparts.

Hands held tight through storms we face,
In this rhythm, find our place.
Together, weaving dreams anew,
A melody in shades of blue.

Thus we wander, side by side,
In a dance where love won't hide.
Timbral trails that softly bind,
Creating harmony, intertwined.

Whirls of Whimsy and Worry

In the garden where laughter grows,
Whirls of whimsy scatter like prose.
Childlike dreams in vibrant hues,
Coloring paths one may choose.

Yet within this playful art,
Worries linger, close to the heart.
A balancing act, light and dark,
Navigating through each spark.

Each twist and turn, a fragile line,
With joy and concern intertwined.
Finding solace in uncertainty,
Whirls of emotion, wild and free.

We learn to dance in the fray,
Embrace the whims that come our way.
Together we'll face each storm,
In these whirls, we find our form.

Threads of the Incongruous

In twilight's glow, shadows dance,
A tapestry of chance and circumstance.
Whispers of dreams woven tight,
Fraying edges in the fading light.

The colors clash, like night and day,
In silence, the contradictions play.
Each thread tells a tale untold,
A paradox in fibers bold.

Here laughter meets the weight of tears,
Echoes of lost and fading years.
We find the beauty in the wrong,
A melody of life, where we belong.

So let us stitch our stories deep,
In every fiber, secrets keep.
With every strand, we forge our fate,
In this tapestry, we navigate.

Lullaby of the Lost

Close your eyes and drift away,
To a world where shadows play.
The echoes of the dreams we seek,
In whispers soft, the lost will speak.

Moonlit paths where memories roam,
Find a place that feels like home.
Once embraced, now lost in time,
A lullaby in whispered rhyme.

Dreamers wander through the night,
Chasing glimmers of fading light.
With every sigh, the heart will yearn,
To find the flame, to feel the burn.

So cradle gently every fear,
In dreams, the echoes will draw near.
Lullabies of those we've crossed,
In silent songs, we find the lost.

The Bittersweet Symphony

In the dawn of a fragile morn,
Life plays out, the heart is worn.
Joy and sorrow intertwine,
In melodies both sharp and fine.

Each note a tear, a smile, a sigh,
In every rise, we learn to fly.
The sweetest pain, a love long gone,
In every heartbeat, a haunting song.

Waves of rhythm crash and swell,
Tales of heartache we know too well.
Yet in the midst of all the grief,
Lies the seed of bittersweet relief.

So let us dance with hues of gray,
In symphonies that guide our way.
For in the music, life's refrain,
We find our joy amidst the pain.

Tides of Tension

The ocean breathes, a restless song,
In waves of calm where we belong.
Pulling tides, they rise and fall,
A dance of power, nature's call.

The swell of thoughts, a stormy sea,
In currents deep, we seek to be.
Caught in a whirl, both fierce and wild,
A world of chaos, yet so beguiled.

Each moment hangs, like heavy air,
In silence, we find strength to dare.
The tides may shift, the shore appears,
In every wave, we face our fears.

So let us ride these tides of change,
Embrace the strange, the wide, the range.
For in the ebb, we learn to trust,
In tides of tension, rise we must.

The Tuning Fork of Turmoil

In shadows deep, the echoes ring,
A note of chaos, a bitter sting.
Fingers tremble on the brink,
Where silence shatters, and thoughts sink.

Resonance waves crash, collide,
A symphony where sorrows bide.
The fork, it quivers, hangs in air,
A melody steeped in despair.

Tension mounts, as dreams take flight,
Yet chaos dims the fading light.
Each vibration stirs the soul,
In turmoil's grasp, we lose control.

But from the depths, a whisper flows,
Through tangled strings, hope softly grows.
With every note, we seek to fight,
The tuning fork ignites the night.

Elegy for Lost Whimsy

In a field of shadows, dreams decay,
Once bright and bold, now faint and gray.
The laughter lingers, a ghostly trace,
Of shining moments, lost in space.

The toys lie rusted, stories untold,
Imagination fades, as we grow old.
Each whimsy chased, like fleeting foam,
The heart recalls, but cannot roam.

Once we danced with colors vast,
Now echoes whisper of shadows cast.
The child within, a distant glow,
Yet memories linger, soft and slow.

In every sigh, we mourn the day,
When innocence slipped away.
An elegy sung, through silent tears,
For lost whimsy, through all the years.

Crescendo of the Turbulent Heart

In the heart's chamber, storms arise,
Passions clash beneath the skies.
A symphony of love and pain,
Notes entwined, a sweet disdain.

Fevered rhythms pulse and thrum,
Each heartbeat echoes, a frantic drum.
Whispers merge in a haunting song,
Where right and wrong both belong.

As crescendos crash in wild embrace,
The shadows dance in a frenzied chase.
Hope and sorrow intertwine tight,
Painting the canvas of restless night.

Yet through the chaos, a melody flows,
Bringing light where the dark wind blows.
In every thunder, serenity breathes,
A turbulent heart that never leaves.

Overture to the Unraveled Self

In the silence, truths unfurl,
An overture to the inner whirl.
Threads of purpose fray and break,
Awakening dreams of what's at stake.

A journey embarked, through tangled lanes,
Chasing echoes where the spirit wanes.
With every step, the layers shed,
Revealing facets of pain and dread.

Reflections murmur in fractured glass,
A tapestry woven of moments passed.
With courage found in the rawest part,
We sift through fragments, reclaim the heart.

Each note a promise, a whisper, a call,
To rise again, despite the fall.
The overture plays, unyielding and true,
In unraveling self, we start anew.

Jagged Notes of a Soft Serenade

In twilight's grasp, the shadows dance,
With whispered tones, they weave romance.
A melody of hearts entwined,
In every note, a secret signed.

The strings may clash, but beauty's found,
In jagged paths, love's echoes sound.
A song that sways with gentle might,
Turns darkness into radiant light.

Through rusted keys, the music flares,
In soft serenades, the heart declares.
Each painful strum, a brush with grace,
In harmony, we find our place.

So linger here, where chaos sings,
The jagged notes, they teach us wings.
In every crack, a chance to soar,
A soft serenade forevermore.

The Paradox of Passion

In fire's glow, we ignite the night,
A dance of souls, both wrong and right.
With fervent hearts, we chase the flame,
Yet fear the burn, and play the game.

Desire burns with a fierce delight,
But shadows linger, haunting the light.
We crave the edge where love resides,
In every joy, a small divide.

The paradox, a bittersweet song,
Where tender whispers don't feel wrong.
In passion's grip, we lose our way,
A tangled fate, come what may.

Yet still we strive, we seek the thrill,
Embrace the chaos, close the chill.
For in this dance, both fierce and meek,
The truth of love is what we seek.

Echoing Emptiness

In hollow halls where silence reigns,
A whisper fades, and nothing gains.
The echoes linger, softly roam,
A distant call we'll never own.

Moments lost in time's cruel hands,
A fleeting grasp, like shifting sands.
The heartbeats fade, a ghostly sound,
In empty spaces, hope is drowned.

Yet still we reach for what is lost,
Through echoes sweet, we count the cost.
In every sigh, a chance to heal,
A silent song that we can feel.

So let the emptiness surround,
For in the void, our strength is found.
In echoes soft, we'll learn to grow,
From darkest nights, true light will flow.

Fluid Frequencies

In waves of sound, emotions flow,
A current strong, we ride the show.
Each note cascades like water clear,
Embracing hearts, dissolving fear.

Fluid frequencies entwine our souls,
Creating rhythms, making us whole.
Within the stream, we find our place,
In every pulse, a warm embrace.

From gentle ripples to crashing tides,
The music swells, it never hides.
In harmony, we dance and sway,
A fluid bond that lights the way.

So let the waves take us afar,
In rhythmic whispers, we are stars.
In fluid frequencies, we unite,
A song of life, pure and bright.

Trackless Journeys in a Melodic Maze

Through winding paths we softly tread,
A symphony of whispers near our head.
Each note a star, each chord a sigh,
In this maze of sound, we learn to fly.

The echoes dance, they twist and twine,
In secret corners, our hearts align.
The journey unwinds, yet never ends,
In the music, our spirit transcends.

We trace the rhythm, the beats unfurl,
With every pulse, we spin and whirl.
Lost yet found, in every refrain,
Trackless journeys, freedom from pain.

In melodies soft, our dreams arise,
A tapestry woven before our eyes.
We move as one, in dreamlike haze,
Through trackless journeys, we chart our gaze.

The Dichotomy of Solitude and Connection

In silence, thoughts begin to swell,
A quiet echo, a private bell.
Solitude wraps in a gentle embrace,
Yet yearnings to share fill empty space.

Connections sought in the darkest night,
A flicker of hope, a guiding light.
Though alone, we reach for the unknown,
In every silence, a love is sown.

The heartbeats sync in a tender dance,
Solitude's song leads to a chance.
In isolation, we find our song,
Realizing together we truly belong.

The ebb and flow, a deepening tide,
With every pulse, we must decide.
To cherish solitude, yet connect with grace,
In this dichotomy, we find our place.

Symphony of Fading Echoes

In the twilight, shadows softly blend,
Whispers of time, they twist and wend.
Each echo lingers, a story untold,
In fading light, the world turns gold.

The orchestra plays, a haunting refrain,
Notes like raindrops, falling like pain.
As memories fade, they weave through the air,
A symphony crafted from love and despair.

Time hushes, as echoes softly call,
An orchestra's heartbeat, a rise and fall.
In the silence, we learn to recall,
The symphony's beauty, that encloses all.

As night descends, the music will wane,
Yet in our souls, its warmth will remain.
In fading echoes, we find our peace,
A symphony that will never cease.

Resonance of Reverie

In the quiet depths of a wandering mind,
Dreams flutter gently, their paths entwined.
With every thought, a new world glows,
In the realm of reverie, anything flows.

Colors blend in a vibrant dance,
Whispers of magic, a fleeting chance.
Our fantasies stretch beyond the known,
In this resonance, seeds are sown.

Elusive visions, both bright and deep,
Awakening wonders that beckon to sleep.
As echoes twist in a delicate thread,
In reverie's charm, we leap and tread.

Each heartbeat pulses with dreams in flight,
Lost in the beauty of fragrant night.
In this space where our spirits play,
Resonance of reverie guides the way.

Chords of Longing and Lament

In shadows deep, the echoes sigh,
A melody that whispers nigh.
With every note, a teardrop falls,
A symphony where silence calls.

The heartstrings pull, a mournful tune,
Beneath the watchful, waning moon.
Each chord a memory, bittersweet,
In solitude, our sorrows meet.

The music swells, a haunting wail,
In every breath, a ghostly trail.
We dance with shadows, lost in time,
A requiem that feels like rhyme.

Yet hope in strings still finds a way,
To lift the veil of night to day.
Through longing's ache, a light appears,
In chords of love, we drown our fears.

The Pulse of Peculiar Thoughts

In the corners of the mind, they creep,
Thoughts that swirl, and thoughts that leap.
Like shadows cast in daylight's glare,
A dance of whispers, light as air.

They flit and float, an errant breeze,
Curious knaves, they never cease.
In tangled webs, they brew and stew,
Painting worlds that feel so new.

The heart beats strong, a wild drum,
Each beat a sign of all they've become.
In the vast expanse of wonder's reach,
Life's peculiar lessons, they teach.

Through silent hours and restless dreams,
The pulse of thoughts in twilight beams.
They linger long, elusive, fleet,
In every mind, they find their seat.

Duets with Doubt

A whisper soft, a tremor near,
In shadows, doubt has drawn so clear.
It weaves through days, and nights it haunts,
In quiet moments, still it taunts.

Two voices clash, like wind and rain,
A battle waged, both joy and pain.
In harmony, they twist and turn,
In echoes sharp, the lessons learn.

Yet in the strife, a truth will rise,
Amidst the fog, the heart's reprise.
For every note of fear we sing,
A counterpoint of courage brings.

With hands entwined, we face the void,
In duets bold, our doubt destroyed.
Together strong, we find the light,
In every shadow, hope takes flight.

Fantasia on Frayed Dreams

In twilight's blush, dreams softly fray,
Threads of yearning, they drift away.
A tapestry of hopes once bright,
Now whispers lost in fading light.

They dance like stars on winter's breath,
In fragments caught, a taste of death.
Yet in the night, they shimmer still,
A flicker of heart, a gentle thrill.

In every sigh, a story lingers,
Spun from the loom of fate's own fingers.
Through tangled paths, a vision weaves,
A fantasy that never leaves.

Embrace the frayed, the torn, the torn,
For in those pieces, dreams are born.
With open hearts, we weave anew,
A fantasia in vibrant hue.

Symphony of Surreal Whispers

In shadows where the dreamers play,
The echoes dance, a soft ballet.
Whispers weave through twilight's veil,
Each note a story, soft and frail.

Beneath the moon's enchanting glow,
Fantastical sights begin to flow.
Reality bends, twirling free,
A tapestry of mystery.

Chimeras laugh, the stars align,
In this realm where souls entwine.
Melodies float, like gentle streams,
Carrying secrets, fragile dreams.

As dawn approaches, still we glide,
In this surreal, wondrous ride.
The symphony fades, yet remains,
A haunting echo that sustains.

Melodies of the Misunderstood

In crowded rooms, I stand alone,
A heart that sings a silent tone.
Words they fail, emotions clash,
Like fleeting shadows, here, then flash.

The notes I play are soft and low,
A language only dreamers know.
Chords of sorrow, chords of grace,
Woven tightly, time won't erase.

Through tangled paths, my spirit roams,
Seeking solace, finding homes.
Each melody a plea for light,
In the darkness, seeking flight.

With every strum, a story grows,
In the rhythms, deep, it flows.
Misunderstood, yet still I sing,
Hoping warmth these notes may bring.

Crescendo of Conflicting Emotions

A tempest brews within my chest,
Quiet calm meets stormy jest.
In perfect harmony, I drown,
Each wave a frown, each smile a crown.

The laughter chokes, the silence screams,
Conflicting tales weave through my dreams.
I dance on edges, sharp and frayed,
In chaos bold, my heart displayed.

Heartbeats clash, an urgent race,
Time unwinds in frantic pace.
Each heartbeat holds a clash of souls,
In hidden depths, emotion rolls.

But out of this chaotic strife,
Emerges strength, a vibrant life.
A crescendo built on stark divides,
Where love and fear together bide.

Harmonies from the Heart's Chamber

In chambers deep where echoes dwell,
Resonating tales the heart must tell.
A symphony of love and pain,
Layered softly, like gentle rain.

Each note a heartbeat, pure and true,
Melodies crafted just for you.
In whispered tones, the secrets flow,
A rhythmic pulse, a vibrant glow.

Harmonies rise, they intertwine,
A dance of souls, a sacred line.
Through every rise and every fall,
The heart composes, answering the call.

In the stillness, listen close,
Feel the warmth that music boasts.
From the depths of love's embrace,
Harmonies bloom, a sacred space.

Cacophony of Cravings

Echoes of hunger pierce the night,
Desires dance in wild delight.
Each whisper calls, a siren's song,
Pulling me where I don't belong.

A taste of sweetness, sharp despair,
Every bite a fleeting prayer.
Savoring chaos, I lose control,
Cravings feast upon my soul.

Fleeting flavors haunt my dreams,
In every corner, hunger screams.
The noise of want invades my mind,
In this cacophony, I'm confined.

Amidst the turmoil, I seek peace,
Yet every moment feels like a lease.
A banquet laid, but never enough,
In this cacophony, life is tough.

Agony in Allegretto

Notes fall softly, heavy with pain,
A melody mourns, a gentle reign.
Rhythms of sorrow, a heart's protest,
Each beat an echo, never at rest.

In every staccato, a longing cries,
Fading whispers, as hope slowly dies.
The tempo dances, but feet are slow,
In this allegretto, darkness will grow.

An aching chorus, shadows align,
Sorrowful strings weave tales divine.
The music lingers, heavy and stark,
Embracing the void, igniting the dark.

With every crescendo, the heart breaks free,
Yet still tethered to painful decree.
In agony's grip, we find our way,
In allegretto, we forever sway.

Weaving Melodies from Sorrow

Threads of grief entwined in song,
Each note a memory, where I belong.
Weaving tales of heartache and strife,
In the fabric of music, I find my life.

Frayed edges whisper stories untold,
Of joy and longing, of dreams grown cold.
Melodies linger like a gentle sigh,
Embracing the pain, letting it fly.

Woven in rhythm, the heart's lament,
Notes like raindrops, each a torment.
Yet from the sorrow, beauty will rise,
In every refrain, a hopeful surprise.

Through darkness, I gather the light,
Crafting a symphony, taking flight.
In weavings of sorrow, joy will unfold,
A tapestry vibrant, a story retold.

The Soloist of Shadows

In the quiet, a figure stands tall,
A soloist hidden, embracing the fall.
Shadows whisper secrets, dark and deep,
In silence, the shadows begin to weep.

With each breath, a haunting refrain,
Melodies linger, echoing pain.
Solitude dances, a partner in crime,
In this shadowed ballet, I lose track of time.

Fingers graze strings of ethereal night,
Crafting a symphony, banishing fright.
A soloist breathes life into gloom,
In the darkness, the heart finds its room.

The shadows applaud with a soft, sweet sigh,
As the soloist sings, I start to fly.
From the depths of despair, a voice will rise,
In the solitude, the spirit defies.

Cadence of Confusion

In whispers lost, a mind does race,
Twisted thoughts, a tangled space.
Echoes bounce, seeking the light,
In shadows deep, fades day to night.

Words that break, then softly blend,
Chasing beats, as feelings bend.
A lullaby of clashing dreams,
Where nothing's real, or so it seems.

Step by step, a path unclear,
Solitude sings, yet feels so near.
Chasing answers in the dark,
Hoping to find a single spark.

But within the chaos, clarity flows,
In the maze of thoughts, wisdom grows.
As confusion swirls, a dance unfolds,
In the heart of storms, truth is bold.

Strings of Solitude

A single note in empty halls,
Resonates as silence calls.
Plucked from depths where shadows lie,
Lonely echoes start to sigh.

The world outside, a distant view,
Connected still, yet far from you.
Each melody, a whispered prayer,
Searching for the warmth of care.

As strings vibrate, emotions soar,
A symphony of less is more.
In solitude, we find our grace,
In every note, a soft embrace.

Moments slip like grains of sand,
In stillness, we take a stand.
Through silence, beauty starts to bloom,
On strings of solitude, we find room.

Vibrations of Hidden Laughter

In corners dark, joy tries to creep,
Silenced smiles that secrets keep.
A chuckle soft, a glance that's sly,
In hidden nooks, where shadows lie.

Ripples dance on calmest seas,
Beneath the surface, playful tease.
Giggling whispers fill the air,
An echo here, a snicker there.

In silent rooms, voices blend,
Old tales of mirth that never end.
With every sigh, a story's told,
In laughter's grip, hearts unfold.

Though hidden well, it's ever near,
The sound of joy, distinct and clear.
In life's embrace, together we roam,
Vibrations of laughter, a home.

The Rhapsody of Restless Minds

Thoughts collide like storms at sea,
A symphony of chaos, wild and free.
Fleeting moments, time slips fast,
In restless waves, futures cast.

Dreams awaken, flutter, and fly,
Chasing the stars that light the sky.
With every pulse, a rhythm found,
In restless hearts, a yearning sound.

Ideas whirl like autumn leaves,
In quiet corners, a mind believes.
Crafting stories from thin air,
The rhapsody sings, beyond despair.

In restless minds, creation brews,
A tapestry of thoughts and views.
With every beat, a life designed,
In the rhapsody of restless minds.